LORD RAMA

Om
SHAKTI
An Imprint of Om Books International

Om SHAKTI An Imprint of Om Books International

Reprinted in 2026

Corporate & Editorial Office
A-12, Sector 64, Noida 201 301
Uttar Pradesh, India
Phone: +91 120 477 4100
Email: editorial@ombooks.com
Website: www.ombooksinternational.com

Sales Office
107, Ansari Road, Darya Ganj
New Delhi 110 002, India
Phone: +91 11 4000 9000
Email: sales@ombooks.com

ISBN: 978-81-19749-46-1

Printed in India

10 9 8 7 6 5 4 3 2

Contents

Birth of Rama

Ayodhya, located on the banks of the Sarayu river, was the capital city of the greatest kingdom of India, Kosala. Ruled by the wise King Dasharatha, it was a prosperous kingdom and the king treated all his subjects as his own children.

Sadly, King Dasharatha was childless. Taking the advice of his council of ministers and wise sages, he took part in the *Putrakamesti* yagna so that the gods could bless him with a son who could carry on the name of the dynasty and rule Ayodhya after him.

The gods, pleased with his dedication, blessed King Dasharatha, and gave him a bowl of rice pudding, which he was asked to give among his three wives, namely—Queen Kaushalya, Queen Sumitra and Queen Kaikeyi.

The blessed rice pudding was shared among the three queens, and soon, the grand palace of Ayodhya was blessed with four princes.

There was much joy and celebrations in the land. With time, the palace was filled with the innocent smiles of the little boys on whom everyone doted.

Dasharatha's eldest son, Rama, was born to Queen Kaushalya, Bharata was born to Queen Kaikeyi and the twins, Lakshmana and Shatrughna, were born to Queen Sumitra.

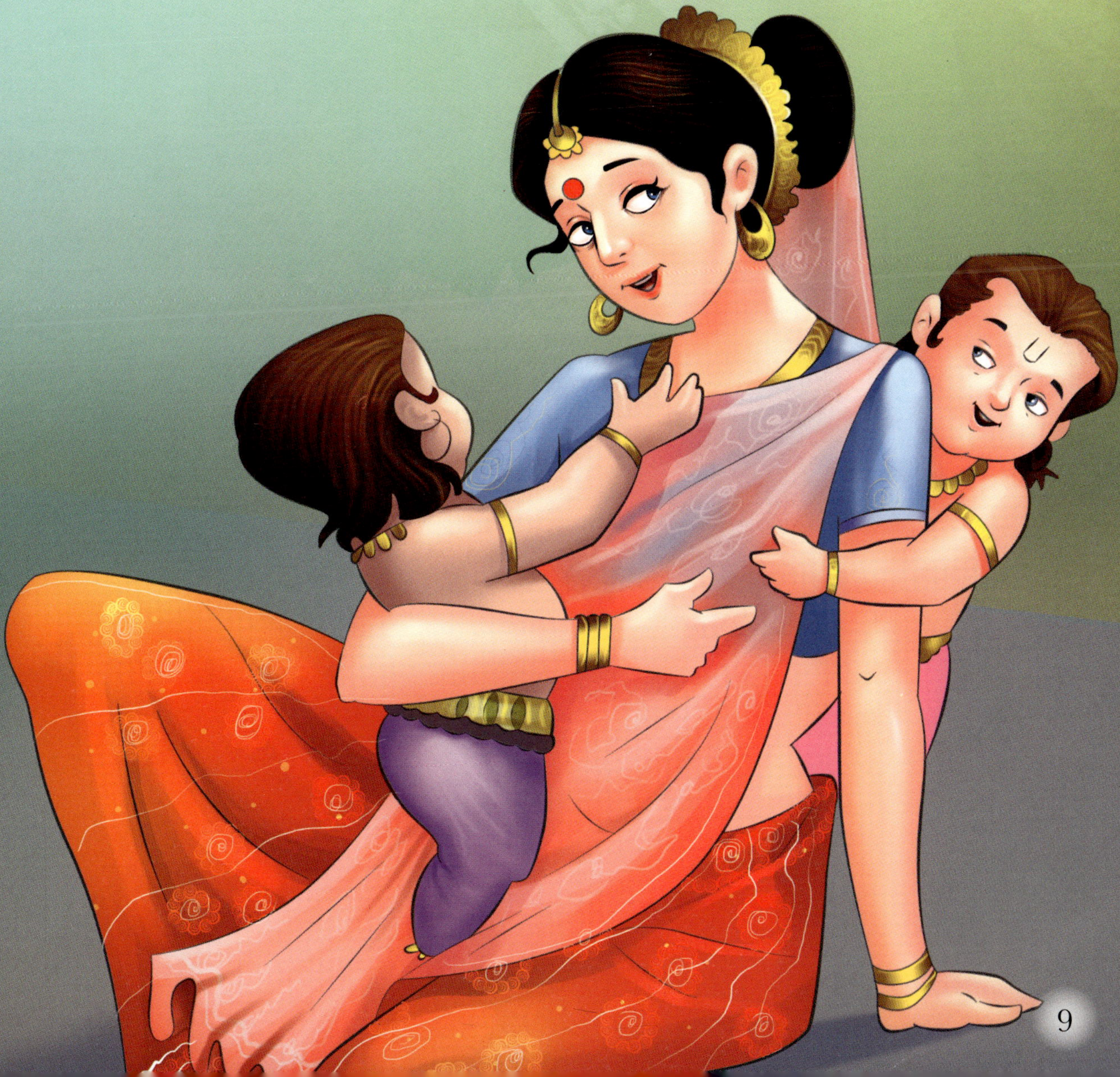

The young princes were always together while they were growing up and they loved each other very much. Even the queen mothers never discriminated among their sons, and loved them all equally. As they grew up, Rama and Lakshmana grew closer and fonder of each other and became inseparable.

King Dasharatha, who was considered to be a master in the art of warfare, sent the four princes to the ashram of Rishi Vashishtha to acquire the skills essential for a prince.

Under his guidance, all the princes mastered archery, mace fighting and the various strategies of war.

Rama's prowess in archery and all the other skills required for a true warrior were unmatched and King Dasharatha was proud with the way his son was proving to be an excellent heir to the throne of Ayodhya.

Rama Defeats Tadaka

Even as peace reigned in Ayodhya, the sages in the Dandaka Forest who were conducting yagnas, were being constantly attacked by the demons.

The lives of the poor people were at the mercy of the demons who harrassed them in every field of life. Not knowing what to do, all of them went to Sage Vishvamitra for help.

Sage Vishvamitra reflected and said, "This seems like the handiwork of the demoness Tadaka. There is only one person in this world who can kill her and bring peace to the forest. I must go to King Dasharatha and ask for the help of his son, Rama."

Everyone feared Tadaka who was a cruel and scary demoness.

King Dasharatha received Sage Vishvamitra very happily. However, when the sage informed him the reason for his visit, the poor king was distraught.

He pleaded with Sage Vishvamitra, "My Lord, please allow me to go and kill Tadaka. Rama is too young. How can he overpower her?"

It was then that Sage Vishvamitra informed him, "Your son is no mere mortal. He is an avatar of Lord Vishnu. I have come to ask for his help because he is the only one who can kill her."

King Dasharatha finally relented, and Rama prepared to go to the forest.

On Lakshmana's insistence, Sage Vishvamitra took both brothers with him.

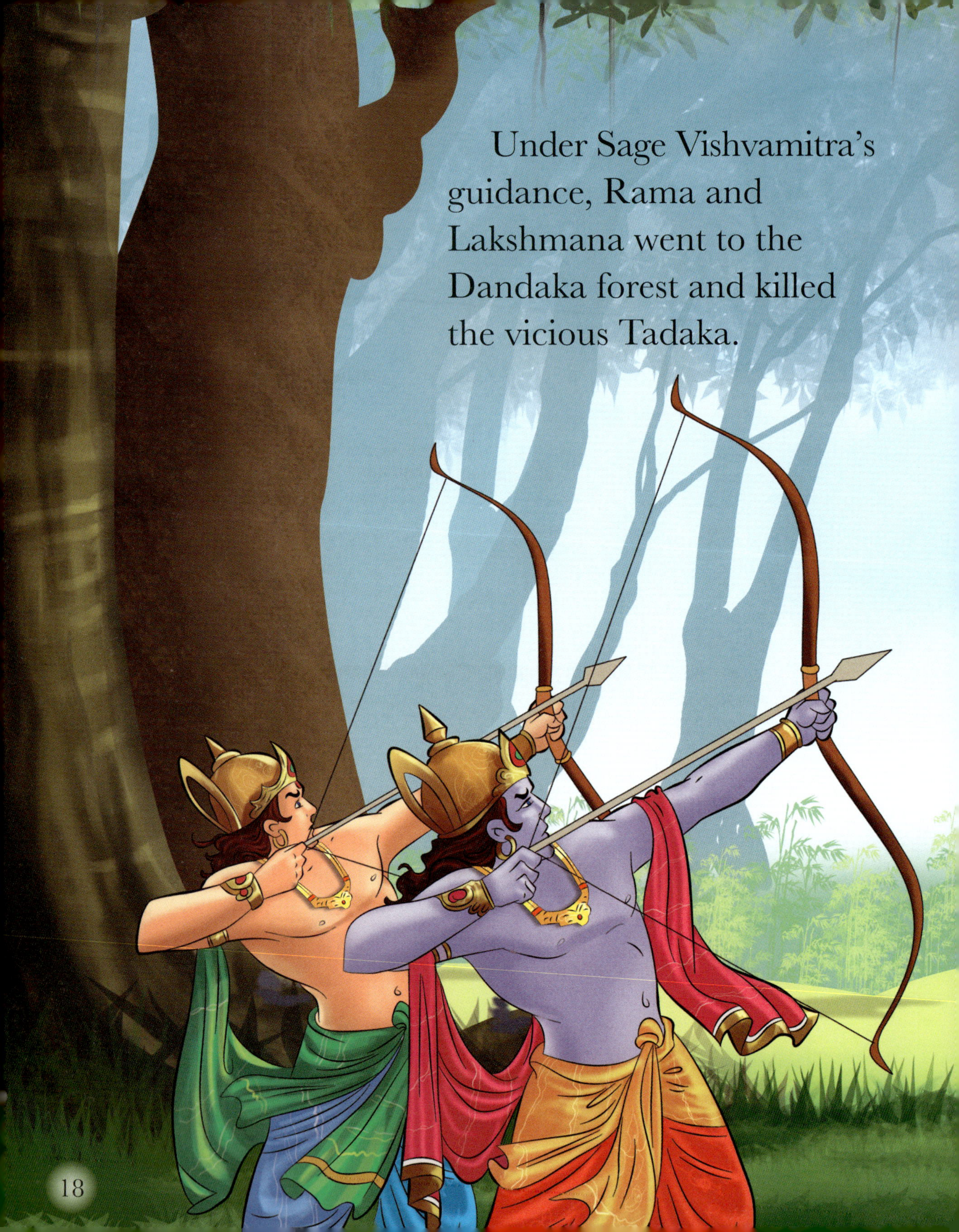

Under Sage Vishvamitra's guidance, Rama and Lakshmana went to the Dandaka forest and killed the vicious Tadaka.

They also defeated the other demons in the forest. The sages could resume their yagnas and peace prevailed in the forest once again.

Sage Vishvamitra was very happy and said, "You two are very brave princes who have helped in defeating the demons in the forest. I would like you to accompany me further on my journey."

Rama and Lakshmana agreed at once.

Rama Marries Sita

When Sage Vishvamitra and the brothers were passing through the kingdom of Mithila, they learnt that the king of Mithila, King Janaka, was holding the *swayamvara* of his daughter, Sita.

It was said that the one who could string the bow of Lord Shiva, would win Sita's hand in marriage. On the sage's insistence, both princes agreed to participate in the *swayamvara*.

The sage knew that the bow was waiting to be broken by Rama and that Sita was destined to marry Rama.

On the day of the swayamvara, many princes arrived to attempt stringing the divine bow. However, no one succeeded.

Finally, it was Rama's turn. A hushed silence fell across the entire court when Rama effortlessly lifted the bow, and then proceeded to string it.

However, the moment he tried to string the ends of the bow, it split into two with a loud, reverberating noise.

King Janaka was very happy. He knew that the prince of Ayodhya was no ordinary man. He was glad that his daughter had finally found a husband worthy of her.

The news of Rama's upcoming marriage to Sita spread like wildfire and an exalted King Dasharatha quickly arrived with his family and subjects to Mithila for the wedding.

Rama married Sita with great pomp and splendour.

The celebrations lasted in both the kingdoms for many, many days.

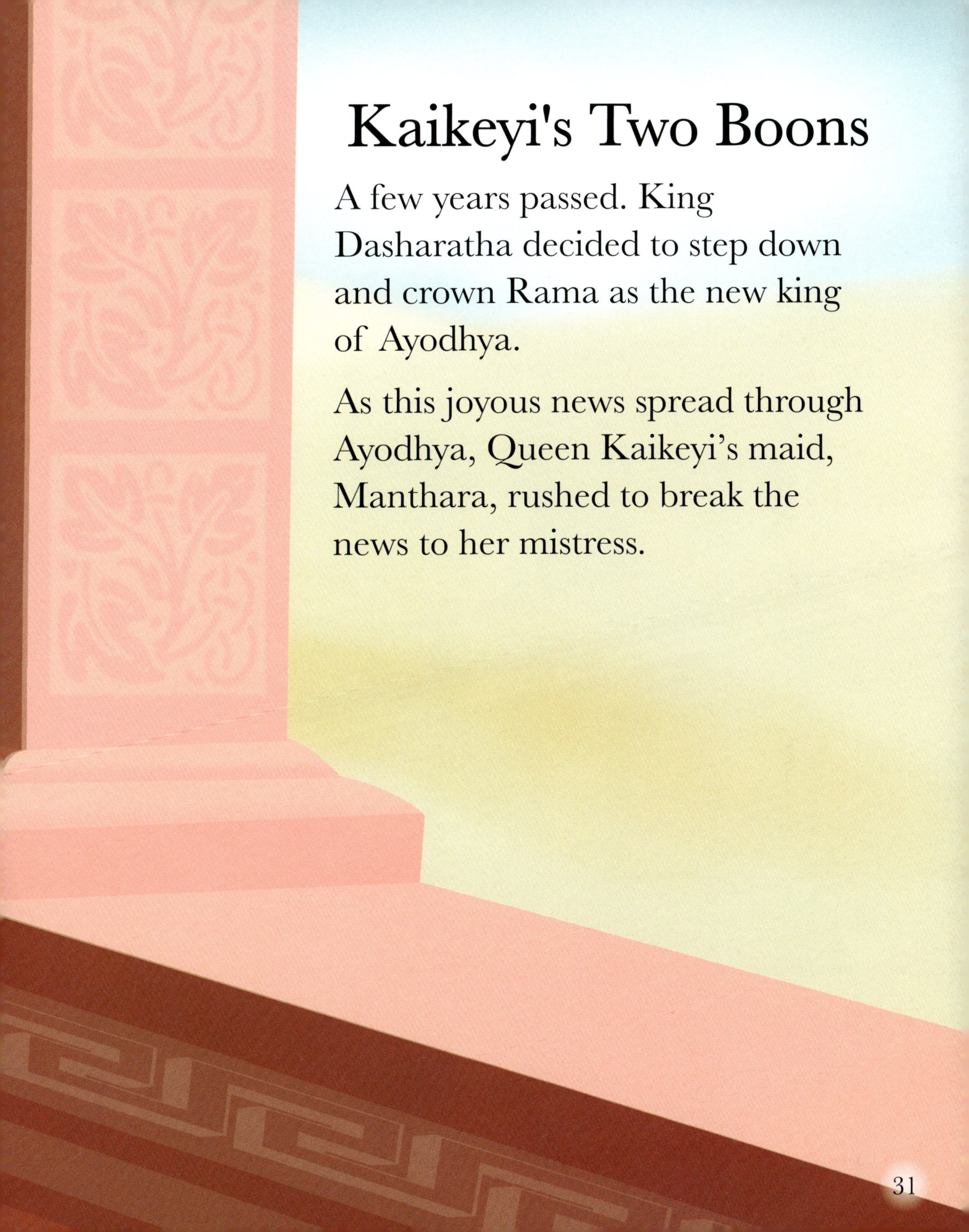

Kaikeyi's Two Boons

A few years passed. King Dasharatha decided to step down and crown Rama as the new king of Ayodhya.

As this joyous news spread through Ayodhya, Queen Kaikeyi's maid, Manthara, rushed to break the news to her mistress.

The devious Manthara tried to poison Queen Kaikeyi's mind against Rama.

She told the queen, "Do you remember that King Dasharatha had given you two boons many years ago? Now is the time to claim those boons for if Rama becomes king, you and Bharat will have no place in the palace."

Queen Kaikeyi replied, “Yes, once I had saved his life in a battle, and when he returned, King Dasharatha granted me two boons and I had told him that I would ask for them when the right time comes.”

“You are right. Now it is time to ask for those two boons,” Manthara suggested.

Manthara immediately added, "Yes, now is the time. Ask the king for the boons. First, he should appoint Bharata as the next king of Ayodhya and second, King Dasharatha should exile Rama to the forest for fourteen years."

Kaikeyi came totally under the influence of Manthara's evil mind and agreed to do whatever she suggested.

Acting as per Manthara's evil schemes, Queen Kaikeyi sent for King Dasharatha.

When he arrived, he found Kaikeyi, weeping. "What is the matter, my dear?" asked the king, as he tried to console his wife. Queen Kaikeyi replied, "My Lord, I want you to grant me the two boons that you had once promised me."

And saying so, she mentioned her conditions to King Dasharatha.

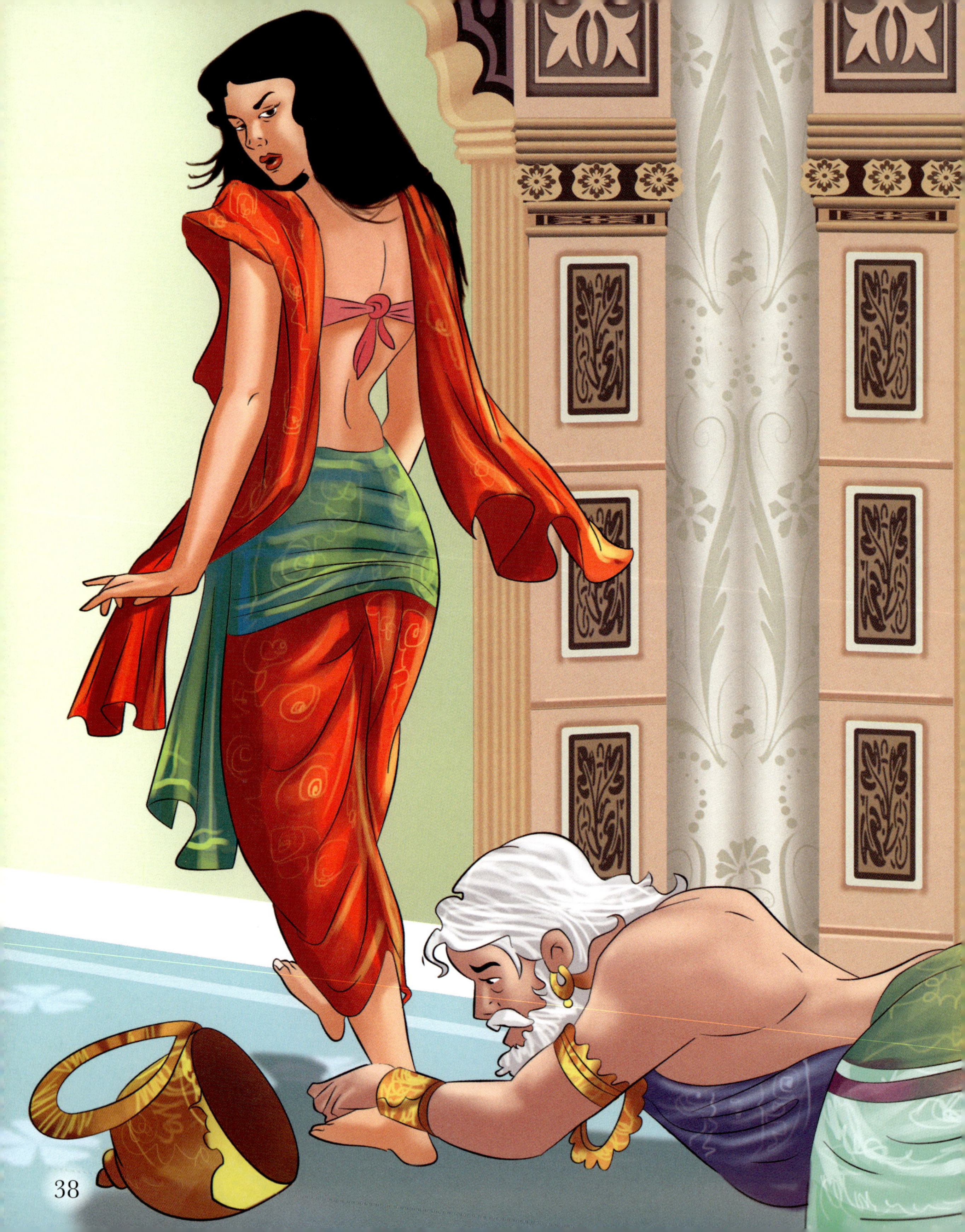

The king was shocked by his wife's request. He pleaded with her to ask him for anything else, but Queen Kaikeyi remained adamant.

Reluctantly the king agreed. He belonged to the Raghukul dynasty which firmly believed that it was better to embrace death than break a promise.

He was beside himself with grief. He shed copious tears and died of a broken heart after sending Ram to exile.

Rama's Exile

When Rama heard about Queen Kaikeyi's demands, he went to King Dasharatha and said, "Father, as you have given your word to Mother Kaikeyi, we must do as she wishes. I will gladly go to the forest and I would be very happy if Bharata is coronated as the future king of Ayodhya."

As Rama made preparations to leave for the forest, Sita said, “My Lord, if you are going to live a life of austerity in the forest, how can I stay in this luxurious palace? I will come with you.”

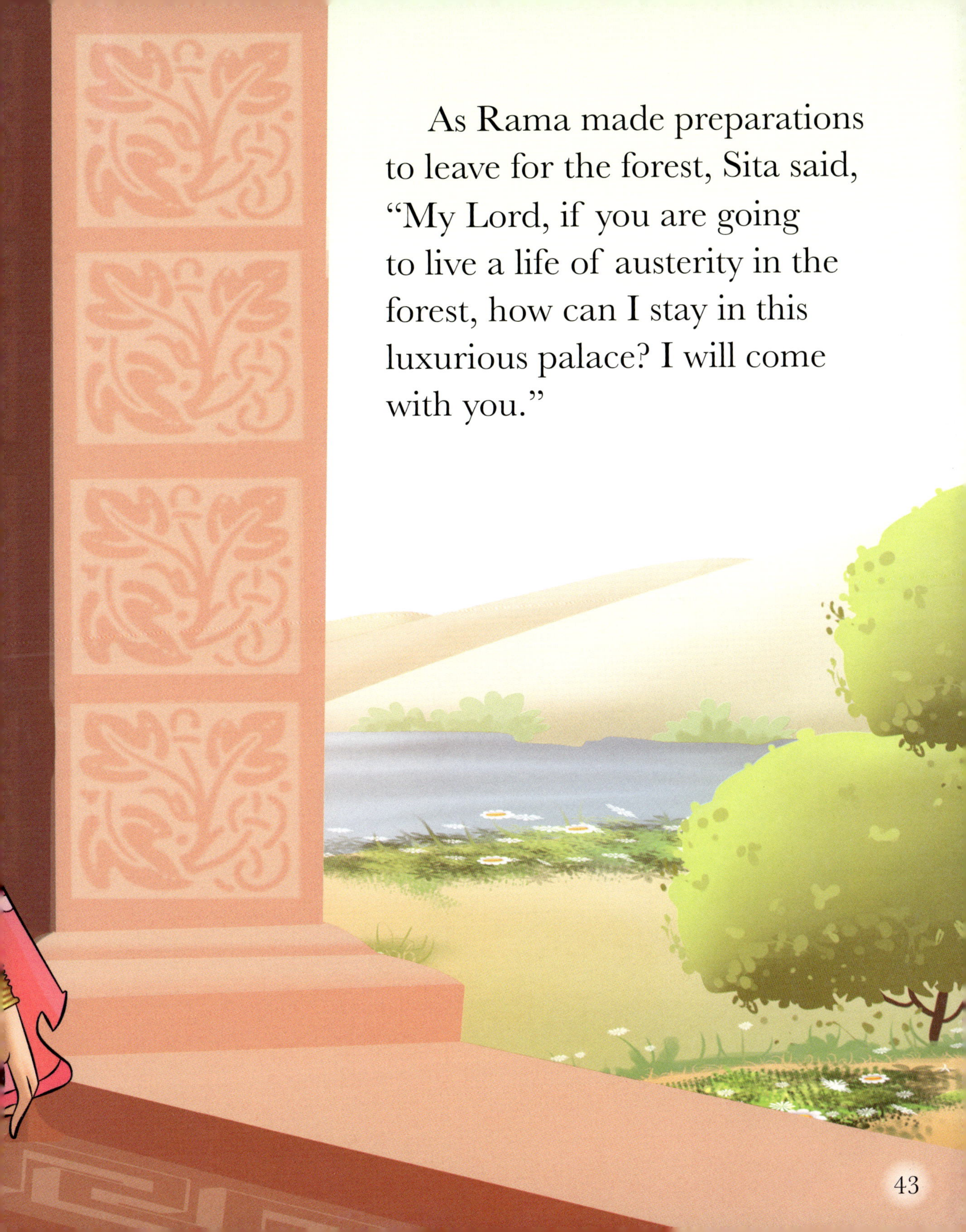

When the news reached Lakshmana, he too sought his brother's permission to accompany them to the exile.

Seeking the blessings from their elders, Rama, along with Sita and Lakshmana, donned the attire of ascetics and left for the forest from Ayodhya.

Bharata's Plea

After travelling deep into the forest, the exiled princes of Ayodhya built a small hut for themselves at a place called Panchavati, where they began to live in happiness and peace.

One day, Rama saw a huge cloud of dust approaching them from the direction of Ayodhya.

On Rama's orders, Lakshmana quickly climbed a tree and announced,"Brother, Bharata is coming, and it seems he is bringing the entire army with him."

When Bharata reached Panchavati, he immediately fell on Rama's feet and pleaded, "Dear brother, Mother Kaikeyi has greatly wronged you. Please accept my apology on her behalf and come back to rule the kingdom that is rightfully yours."

Rama smiled at his brother and said, "No, Bharata, I must live in the forest for fourteen years as per Mother Kaikeyi's wish. Otherwise, I will be disobeying her orders. My love and loyalty for her and our father is way more than my desire to be the king. You must return at once and rule Ayodhya wisely."

Bharata reluctantly accepted his elder brother's orders.

However, before he left, he took Rama's slippers and declared, "I shall do as you ask, Brother, but till the time you return and accept the throne that is rightfully yours, I shall place your sandals on it and rule under your guidance."

Surpanakha

Rama's peaceful life in the forest did not last for long. One day when Surpanakha, the demoness sister of Ravana, king of Lanka, was passing through the forest, her eyes fell on Rama.

Enchanted by his divine looks, she at once fell in love with him and wanted to marry him. With her evil magic powers, she changed her appearance from a demoness to a beautiful woman and appearing before Rama, she said, "O noble stranger! I have fallen in love with you and wish to marry you."

Rama smiled and replied, "I cannot marry you, as I am already married to Sita."

Just as Rama finished speaking, Sita came out of the hut and joined Rama. The demoness went mad on seeing her standing next to Rama, and she turned back into her original form and vowed to seek revenge by killing Sita.

However, just as Surpanakha was about to pounce on Sita, Lakshmana jumped before her and cut her nose off in one quick flash.

She ran away, howling and threatening to take revenge.

Surpanakha ran straight to Ravana's court. "An evil man called Rama is living in the forest and has attacked your sister. You have to avenge my insult."

Ravana was furious. He called his uncle Maricha and said, "Tomorrow, you will assume the form of a golden deer and lure Rama out of his hut. Remember to call out to Lakshmana in Rama's voice and once Sita is left all alone in her hut, I will abduct her."

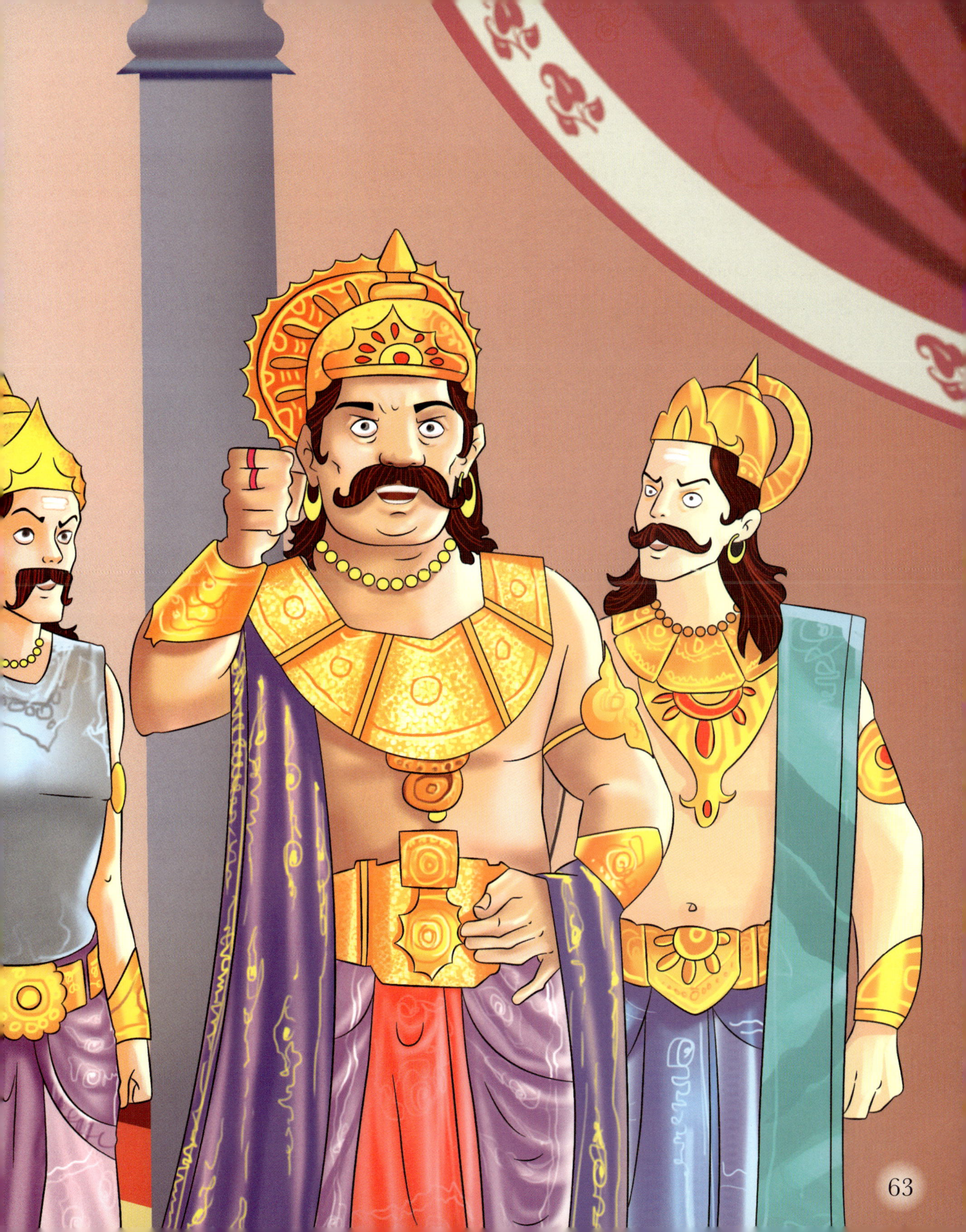

Sita's Abduction

The next day, as Sita was sitting in the courtyard, she saw a beautiful golden deer leap past the hut. "My dear husband, I have never seen a deer like that in my life. Could you please catch it for me?" With a smile on his lips, Rama immediately grabbed his bow and arrow and set off after the deer. But moments later, Sita heard Rama call out, "Lakshmana, help!" Sita turned to Lakshmana and said, "Go and help your brother!"

Lakshmana did not want to leave Sita alone, although he was also worried about his brother. But seeing how concerned Sita was about her husband's well-being, Lakshmana drew a *Lakshman Rekha* around their hut and asked Sita, "Please don't step out of this line for any reason till we return."

Then he went out to search for Rama.

No sooner did Lakshmana leave, Ravana came to Sita disguised as a sage and asked for alms.

Sita immediately brought some food for him, but the moment Ravana tried to cross the Lakshman Rekha, his skin burned. "This is most unfair! If you do not want to give me any alms, you should have said so. You have caused me a lot of pain!"

Sita did not want to offend the sage so she stepped out of the line.

No sooner did she do so, Ravana came to his real form and dragged Sita away to his flying chariot.

Rama Meets Hanuman

When Rama and Lakshmana returned to the hut, they were shocked to find Sita missing.

While they were searching for her they came upon an injured Jatayu, the king of vultures and King Dasharatha's friend. He told them, "It was Ravana, the demon king of Lanka who has abducted your wife. I tried my best to save her, but he was too powerful for me."

Rama and Lakshmana immediately set off for Lanka, knowing that they had no other option but to fight Ravana to save Sita.

During their journey, the brothers met the vanara (monkey) chief, Hanuman. On hearing their story Hanuman proposed that if the brothers helped King Sugriva to retrieve his kingdom from the evil King Bali, he, as well as King Sugriva, would help them. Rama helped Sugriva and Hanuman kept his promise. He flew to Lanka to find out Sita's place of confinement in that land.

Rama and Lakshmana, with the support of King Sugriva and his army of monkeys *vanarasena*, decided to attack Lanka.

However, there was one problem—the island of Lanka was separated by the sea from the mainland of India.

The vanaras immediately got busy building a bridge to reach Lanka.

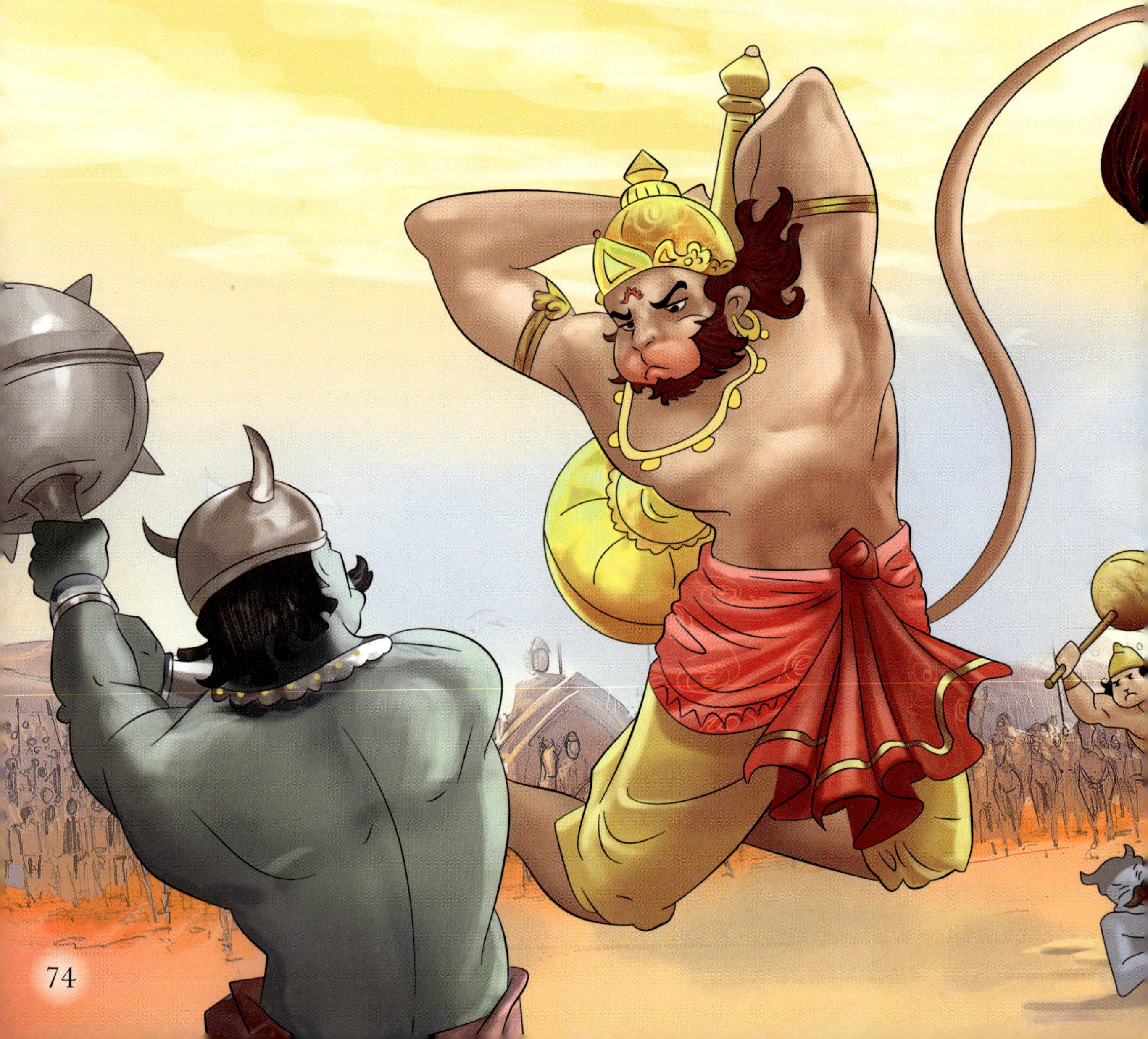

The Final Battle

A fierce battle ensued between the two forces—Rama's army and Ravana's army. Rama and Lakshmana fought bravely against Ravana's army.

Ravana started to panic and sought help from his brother, Kumbhakarna, a giant who spent his time either sleeping or eating.

After Kumbhakarna's failed attempts and death, Indrajit, Ravana's son, used illusion to dupe Rama and ended up injuring Lakshmana.

Hanuman brought *sanjeevani booti*, the magical herb from the Himalayas to save Lakshmana's life. Lakshmana revived and managed to defeat Indrajit.

Finally, Rama and Ravana came face to face. Rama kept firing arrows at Ravana's head, but Ravana used his dark magic to grow ten heads in its place.

All of Rama's special weapons did not affect Ravana. He too had special weapons and attacked Rama.

Vibhishana, Ravana's younger brother, and a spiritual man, came to help Rama.

He told Rama to aim at Ravana's navel, his weak point that would kill him.

After a long battle, finally, Rama defeated Ravana and rescued Sita.

Soon the period of exile ended and Rama, Sita and Lakshmana returned to Ayodhya, where Rama ruled wisely for many years to come.